THE HURTING KIND

THE HURTING KIND

POEMS

ADA LIMÓN

MILKWEED EDITIONS

Published 2022 by Milkweed Editions
Printed in Canada
Cover design by Mary Austin Speaker
Cover artwork by Stacia Brady
Author photo by Lucas Marquardt
22 23 24 25 26   5 4 3 2 1
First Edition

Library of Congress Cataloging-in-Publication Data

Names: Limón, Ada, author.
Title: The hurting kind / Ada Limón.
Description: First Edition. | Minneapolis, Minnesota : Milkweed Editions, 2022. |
    Summary: "An astonishing collection about interconnectedness-between the human
    and nonhuman, ancestors and ourselves-from National Book Critics Circle Award
    winner and National Book Award finalist Ada Limón"-- Provided by publisher.
Identifiers: LCCN 2021050271 (print) | LCCN 2021050272 (ebook) | ISBN
    9781639550494 (hardcover) | ISBN 9781639550500 (ebook)
Subjects: LCGFT: Poetry.
Classification: LCC PS3612.I496 H87 2022 (print) | LCC PS3612.I496 (ebook) | DDC
    811/.6--dc23
LC record available at https://lccn.loc.gov/2021050271
LC ebook record available at https://lccn.loc.gov/2021050272

Milkweed Editions is committed to ecological stewardship. We strive to align our book production
practices with this principle, and to reduce the impact of our operations in the environment. We are a
member of the Green Press Initiative, a nonprofit coalition of publishers, manufacturers, and authors
working to protect the world's endangered forests and conserve natural resources. *The Hurting Kind* was
printed on acid-free 100% postconsumer-waste paper by Friesens Corporation.

For Brady

CONTENTS

I ASK FOR SILENCE

though it's late, though it's night,
and you are not able.

Sing as if nothing were wrong.

Nothing is wrong.

ALEJANDRA PIZARNIK
(TRANSLATED BY YVETTE SIEGERT)

THE HURTING KIND

I.

SPRING

GIVE ME THIS

I thought it was the neighbor's cat, back
to clean the clock of the fledgling robins low
in their nest stuck in the dense hedge by the house,
but what came was much stranger, a liquidity
moving, all muscle and bristle: a groundhog
slippery and waddle-thieving my tomatoes, still
green in the morning's shade. I watched her
munch and stand on her haunches, taking such
pleasure in the watery bites. Why am I not allowed
delight? A stranger writes to request my thoughts
on suffering. Barbed wire pulled out of the mouth,
as if demanding that I kneel to the trap of coiled
spikes used in warfare and fencing. Instead,
I watch the groundhog more closely and a sound escapes
me, a small spasm of joy I did not imagine
when I woke. She is a funny creature and earnest,
and she is doing what she can to survive.

DROWNING CREEK

Past the strip malls and the power plants,
out of the holler, past Gun Bottom Road
and Brassfield and before Red Lick Creek,
there's a stream called Drowning Creek where
I saw the prettiest bird I'd seen all year,
the belted kingfisher, crested in its Aegean
blue plumage, perched not on a high snag
but on a transmission wire, eyeing the creek
for crayfish, tadpoles, and minnows. We were
driving fast toward home and already our minds
were pulled taut like a high black wire latched
to a utility pole. I wanted to stop, stop the car
to take a closer look at the solitary, stocky water
bird with its blue crown and its blue chest
and its uncommonness. But already we were
a blur and miles beyond the flying fisher
by the time I had realized what I'd witnessed.
People were nothing to that bird, hovering over
the creek. I was nothing to that bird, which wasn't
concerned with history's bloody battles or why
this creek was called Drowning Creek, a name
I love though it gives me shivers, because
it sounds like an order, a place where one
goes to drown. The bird doesn't call the creek
that name. The bird doesn't call it anything.
I'm almost certain, though I am certain
of nothing. There is a solitude in this world
I cannot pierce. I would die for it.

SWEAR ON IT

Loosen the thin threads
spooling in the rafters

invisible nests in night's
green offerings, divide

and then divide again.
American linden looming

over the streetlights, so
much taller is the tree,

so much taller is the tree.

SANCTUARY

Suppose it's easy to slip
        into another's green skin,
bury yourself in leaves

and wait for a breaking,
        a breaking open, a breaking
out. I have, before, been

tricked into believing
        I could be both an I
and the world. The great eye

of the world is both gaze
        and gloss. To be swallowed
by being seen. A dream.

To be made whole
        by being not a witness,
but witnessed.

INVASIVE

What's the thin break
inescapable, a sudden thud
on the porch, a phone
vibrating with panic on the night
stand? Bury the broken thinking
in the backyard with the herbs. One
last time, I attempt to snuff out
the fig buttercup, the lesser celandine,
invasive and spreading down
the drainage ditch I call a creek
for a minor pleasure. I can
do nothing. I take the soil in
my clean fingers and to say
I weep is untrue, weep is too
musical a word. I heave
into the soil. You cannot die.
I just came to this life
again, alive in my silent way.
Last night I dreamt I could
only save one person by saying
their name and the exact
time and date. I choose you.
I am trying to kill the fig buttercup
the way I'm supposed to according
to the government website,
but right now there's a bee on it.
Yellow on yellow, two things
radiating life. I need them both
to go on living.

A GOOD STORY

Some days—dishes piled in the sink, books littering the coffee table—
are harder than others. Today, my head is packed with cockroaches,

dizziness, and everywhere it hurts. Venom in the jaw, behind the eyes,
between the blades. Still, the dog is snoring on my right, the cat, on my left.

Outside, all those redbuds are just getting good. I tell a friend, *The body
is so body*. And she nods. I used to like the darkest stories, the bleak

snippets someone would toss out about just how bad it could get.
My stepfather told me a story about when he lived on the streets as a kid,

how he'd, some nights, sleep under the grill at a fast food restaurant until
both he and his buddy got fired. I used to like that story for some reason,

something in me that believed in overcoming. But right now all I want
is a story about human kindness, the way once, when I couldn't stop

crying because I was fifteen and heartbroken, he came in and made
me eat a small pizza he'd cut up into tiny bites until the tears stopped.

Maybe I was just hungry, I said. And he nodded, holding out the last piece.

IN THE SHADOW

The wild pansy shoves its persistent face beneath
      the hackberry's shade, true plum and gold,

with the alternate names: Johnny-jump-up,
      heartsease, or my favorite, love-in-idleness.

I bow closer to the new face. I am always superimposing
      a face on flowers, I call the violet moon vinca

the choir, and there are surely eyes in the birdeye speedwell,
      and mouths on the linearleaf snapdragon.

It is what we do in order to care for things, make them
      ourselves, our elders, our beloveds, our unborn.

But perhaps that is a lazy kind of love. Why
      can't I just love the flower for being a flower?

How many flowers have I yanked to puppet
      as if it was easy for the world to make flowers?

FORSYTHIA

At the cabin in Snug Hollow near McSwain Branch creek, just spring, all the animals are out, and my beloved and I are lying in bed in a soft silence. We are talking about how we carry so many people with us wherever we go, how, even when simply living, these unearned moments are a tribute to the dead. We are both expecting to hear an owl as the night deepens. All afternoon, from the porch, we watched an Eastern towhee furiously build her nest in the untamed forsythia with its yellow spilling out into the horizon. I told him that the way I remember the name *forsythia* is that when my stepmother, Cynthia, was dying, that last week, she said lucidly but mysteriously, *More yellow*. And I thought yes, more yellow, and nodded because I agreed. Of course, more yellow. And so now in my head, when I see that yellow tangle, I say, *For Cynthia, for Cynthia, forsythia, forsythia, more yellow*. It is night now, and the owl never comes. Only more of night, and what repeats in the night.

AND, TOO, THE FOX

Comes with its streak of red
flashing across the lawn, squirrel
bound and bouncing almost
as if it were effortless to hunt,
food being an afterthought or
just a little boring. He doesn't
say a word. Just uses those four
black feet to silently go about
his work, which doesn't seem
like work at all but play. Fox
lives on the edges, pieces together
a living out of leftovers and lazy
rodents too slow for the telephone
pole. He takes only what he needs
and lives a life that some might
call small, has a few friends, likes
the grass when it's soft and green,
never cares how long you watch,
never cares what you need
when you're watching, never cares
what you do once he is gone.

STRANGER THINGS IN THE THICKET

What to root for, what to root for, I rub
      my hands together and eye the surroundings.

Who's gonna win in this blasted waste,
save a nickel and ease the masterclass

           into your own sorrowful palm. She doesn't
           like the word *honey* so she won't like
           the whole song that has honey in its
           chorus. It's cold today so the sun's a lie.

It's all a lie, my closest confidant replies.
      Some raggedy squirrel keeps eating samaras

and scattering their uselessness into the wind.
      I don't know why he is raggedy—could be

fox, could be fence post, something got him.
      Still we see him every year, come to drink

deeply from the birdbath, come to forage
      in the shade of the lilac and mop cypress.

Sure, sure, it's so obvious, that's who to root
for, the thing almost dead

that is, in fact, not
dead at all.

GLIMPSE

In the bathroom our last
cat comes up to me and purrs
even without touch she purrs
and there are times I can
hold her when no one else
can hold her. She once
belonged to my husband's
ex-girlfriend who is no longer
of the earth and what I've
never told him is that some
nights when I touch her
I wonder if the cat is feeling
my touch or just remembering
her last owner's touch. She
is an ancient cat and prickly.
When we are alone I sing
full throated in the empty house
and she meows and mewls
like we've done this before
but we haven't done this before.

THE FIRST LESSON

She took the hawk wing
and spread it

slightly from the shoulder
down, from the bend

of the wing to the lesser
coverts, from the primary coverts

to the tertials, to the carpal edge.
The bird was dead

to begin with, found
splayed over the white

line of Arnold Drive. She was not
scared of death, she took

the bird in like a stray
thing that needed warmth

and water. She pulled it apart
to see how it worked.

My mother nailed the wing
to her studio wall.

She told me not to be
scared. I watched

and learned to watch
closely the world.

ANTICIPATION

Before I dug
the plot
in our yard,
before we had
a yard, when
grass only grew
between stop
signs and garbage
cans, when I
had one pot
for a pepper
and one pot
for a roma
on the fire
escape, I was
planting my
secret seeds
inside you,
the crimson
linen curtains
billowing in
liquid spring
wind, the future
deepening
in the heat.

FOALING SEASON

1.

In the dew-saturated foot-high blades
       of grass, we stand amongst a sea

of foals, mare and foal, mare and foal,
       all over the soft hillside there are twos,

small duos ringing harmoniously in the cold,
       swallows diving in and out, their fabled

forked tail where, the story says, the fireball
       hit it as it flew to bring fire to humanity.

Our friend the Irishman drives us in the Gator
       to sit amongst them. Everywhere doubles

of horses still leaning on each other, still nuzzling
       and curious with each new image.

2.

Two female horses, retired mares, separated
       by a sliding barn door, nose each other.

Neither of them will get pregnant again,
       their job is to just be a horse. Sometimes,

though, they cling to one another, find a friend
       and will whine all night for the friend

to be released. Through the gate, the noses
        touch, and you can almost hear—

Are you okay? Are you okay?

3.

I will never be a mother.

That's all. That's the whole thought.

I could say it returns to me, watching the horses.

Which is true.

But also I could say that it came to me

as the swallows circled us over and over,

something about that myth of their tail,

how generosity is punished by the gods.

But isn't that going too far? I saw a mare

with her foal, and then many mares

with many foals, and I thought, simply:

I will never be a mother.

4.

One foal is a biter, and you must watch
him as he bares his teeth and goes
for the soft spot. He's brilliant, leggy,
and comes right at me, as if directed
by some greater gravity, and I stand
firm, and put my hand out first, rub
the long white marking on his forehead,
silence his need for biting with affection.
I love his selfishness, our selfishness,
the two of us testing each other, swallows
all around us. Every now and then, his
teeth come at me once again; he wants
to teach me something, to get me
where it hurts.

NOT THE SADDEST THING IN THE WORLD

All day I feel some itchiness around
the collar, constriction of living. I write

the date at the top of a letter; though
no one has been writing the year lately,

I write the year, seems like a year you
should write, huge and round and awful.

In between my tasks, I find a dead fledgling,
maybe dove, maybe dunno to be honest,

too embryonic, too see-through and wee.
I don't even mourn him, just all matter-of-

fact-like take the trowel, plant the limp body
with a new hosta under the main feeder.

Seems like a good place for a close-eyed
thing, forever close-eyed, under a green plant

in the ground, under the feast up above. Between
the ground and the feast is where I live now.

Before I bury him, I snap a photo and beg
my brother and my husband to witness this

nearly clear body. Once it has been witnessed
and buried, I go about my day, which isn't

ordinary, exactly, because nothing is ordinary
now even when it is ordinary. Now, something's

breaking always on the skyline, falling over
and over against the ground, sometimes

unnoticed, sometimes covered up like sorrow,
sometimes buried without even a song.

STILLWATER COVE

It seemed a furtive magic—
sun ricocheting off cresting waves near
Stillwater Cove, the soft rock cliffs

of sandstone and clay, the wind-tilted
cypress trees leaning toward
the blue Pacific—and it was only you

who'd see them. A migrating pod
of gray whales going northward, new
calves in tow, shooting a spray of frothy

expelled water from their blowholes
and making a show of breaching
in the clear spring air off the coastline.

We'd whine that we never
caught a glimpse of a slick back or tail slap,
nary a spy-hopping head raised

above the swirling surface. Too young
to look outward for long, we'd lower
our eyes toward what lived small,

the alligator lizard in the coyote brush,
the bracken fern, orange monkey
flower, the beach fly, the earwig, the tick.

It was your trick, always a whale
as soon as our heads went down. Had
to have been a lie: they'd come up

while we zeroed in on Mexican sage
or the monarch. Distracted
by the evidence of life at our feet,

we had no time for the waiting
that was required. To watch
the waves until the whales surfaced

seemed a maddening task. Now, I am
in the inland air that smells of smoke
and gasoline, the trees blown leafless by

wind. Could you refuse me if I asked you
to point again at the horizon, to tell me
something was worth waiting for?

2.
SUMMER

IT BEGINS WITH THE TREES

Two full cypress trees in the clearing
intertwine in a way that almost makes

them seem like one. Until, at a certain angle
from the blue blow-up pool I bought

this summer to save my life, I see it
is not one tree but two, and they are

kissing. They are kissing so tenderly
it feels rude to watch, one hand

on the other's shoulder, another
in the other's branches, like hair.

When did kissing become so
dangerous? Or was it always so?

That illicit kiss in the bathroom
of the Four-Faced Liar, a bar

named after a clock—what was her
name? Or the first one with you,

on the corner of Metropolitan
Avenue, before you came home

with me forever. I watch those green
trees now and it feels libidinous.

I want them to go on kissing, without
fear. I want to watch them and not

feel so abandoned by hands. Come
home. Everything is begging you.

BANISHED WONDERS

The American linden sways nonplussed by the storm,
      a bounce here, a shimmy there, just shaking like music

left over from the night's end wafting into the avenues before sleep.
      I remember once walking down Clinton Street, and singing

that line returning, *New York is cold, but I like where I'm living.*
      There's music on Clinton Street all through the evening. And of course

there was music, though it was me and my incessant remembering.
      And here, now, what does one even offer?

Darling Cockroaches of the Highest Order, hard underthings
      of hard underworlds, I am utterly suspicious of advice.

What is the world like out there? Are you singing in the tunnels?

I should say nothing sometimes.
I should say, *Memory will leap from the mountain.*

      Dearest purple spiderwort in the ditch's mud, how did you do it?
Such bravery, such softness, even with all that name-calling and rage.

No one wants to be a pretty thing all the time. But no one wants to be
      the weed. Alone in Argentina at a café, I never felt like dancing, I screwed

my face up so it said nothing and no one and never. Borges lost his sight,
over years, and yet sometimes it is best to be invisible.

What is it to be seen in the right way? As who you are? A flash of color,
      a blur in the crowd,
          something spectacular but untouchable.

And now the world is gone. No more Buenos Aires or Santiago.
      No tango, no samba. No more pisco sours sweet and sticky
and piercing the head's stubborn brick.

Mistral writes: *We don't need all the things that used to give us pleasure.*
      Still some dense desire, to sneak into the cities of the world

again, a window, to sit at Café Tortoni and refuse an invitation
because I can. Now we endure.

Endure time, this envenomed veil of extremes—loss and grief and reckoning.

Mistral writes: *I killed a woman in me: one I did not love.* But I do not want to kill
      that longing woman in me. I love her and I want her to go on longing

until it drives her mad, that longing, until her desire is something

like a blazing flower, a tree shaking off
      the torrents of rain as if it is simply making music.

WHERE THE CIRCLES OVERLAP

We burrow.
We hunch.
We beg and beg.

The thesis is still a river.

At the top of the mountain
is a murderous light, so strong

it's like staring into an original
joy, foundational,

that brief kinship of hold
and hand, the space between

teeth right before they break
into an expansion, a heat.

We hurry.
We hanker.
We beg and beg.

When should we mourn?

We think time is always time.
And place is always place.

Bottlebrush trees attract
the nectar lovers, and we

capture, capture, capture.

The thesis is still the wind.

The thesis has never been exile.
We have never been exiled.
We have been in the sun,

strong and between sleep,
no hot gates, no house decayed,

just the bottlebrush alive
on all sides with want.

WHEN IT COMES DOWN TO IT

Trip the door to stick,
we with the bag mouths

yawping in the blank
space where our joy

once lived, little blooming
weed, purple dead nettle:

where have you gone,
good flourishing? Red

feather I found bent
on the wildflower berm,

soaked but not soaked,
simply shadowed, still,

unweighted, insistent
it belongs to flight.

THE MAGNIFICENT FRIGATEBIRD

Is it okay to begin with the obvious? I am full of stones—
       is it okay not to look out this window, but to look out another?

A mentor once said, *You can't start a poem with a man looking*
       out a window. Too many men looking out a window.

What about a woman? Today is a haunting. One last orange
       on the counter: it is a dead fruit. We swallow dead things.

Once, in Rio near Leblon, large seabirds soared over the vast
       South Atlantic Ocean. I had never seen them before.

Eight-foot wingspan and gigantic in their confident gliding, black,
       with a red neck like a wound or a hidden treasure. Or both.

When I looked it up, I learned it was the Magnificent Frigatebird.
       It sounded like that enormity of a bird had named itself.

What a pleasure to say, *I am Magnificent.* And, too, they traveled as a team,
       so I wondered if they named each other. Generously tapping

one another's deeply forked tail or their plumage, glistening with salt air,
       their gular sacs saying, *You are Magnificent. You are also Magnificent.*

It makes me want to give all my loves the adjectives they deserve:
       You are Resplendent. You are Radiant. You are Sublime.

I am far away from tropical waters. I have no skills for flight or wings
       to skim the waves effortlessly, like the wind itself. But from here,

I can still imagine rapture, a glorious caught fish in the mouth of a bird.

BLOWING ON THE WHEEL

It's getting late, the light's grayish gold
on the hillside and I'm thinking of car rides
from Brooklyn to the Cape, or up
to Moon Mountain from the City,
or out to Stockbridge that one winter
with H and her sister and cousin
and how we called them the Stockbridges.
And I accidentally said, *Have a Norman Mailer*
Christmas and not a Norman Rockwell Christmas
and we laughed at how sad a Norman Mailer
Christmas would be. Or how, another time, we
waited for T to put our bags in the car
as if she was not just driving, but
the driver. Or how after T got a ticket
on 6 East she'd go the speed limit but blow
on the steering wheel like it was a sail and say,
Is the car even on? The three of us,
always piling into the back of some cab
and deciding what was next, which was never bed
because there was still so much to figure out.
And how someone once asked H if we
ever just ran out of subjects to keep
talking about, and of course we wouldn't,
we won't, it's endless, even this is endless,
the sky darkening in the way that makes me
wish we were wandering right now around
New York City somewhere or at the Governor
Bradford and not wandering at all, or just talking or
not talking or being happy or not unhappy,
and this is my secret work, to be worthy

of you both and this infinite discourse
where everything is interesting because you
point it out and say, *Isn't that interesting?*
And how mostly we say, *Remember*
that time, and we will nod because we do
remember that time. Except for the few times
we've forgotten, like that one time when H
was trying to remind us of something and when
we asked her what, she said, *I don't know,*
but you were there and I was there. And we were.

JAR OF SCORPIONS

Translucent and slithering against the beige carpet,
        like a dozen fugitive ideas shoved to the back

of the brain's border—the ideas about hurting yourself
        or hurting others—they came into view, the filaments

of nightmares, the stinging slopsuckers, the venomous miscreants,
        two pedipalps grasping for prey already in the first hours

of their birth. How strange to think that nearly thirty years later, I see
        those nascent scorpions as clear as today's dead moth

stuck to the screen's small squares. We did what children do
        with tiny and terrible things, we trapped them so we could see

more closely, intimately, investigate their particular evildoing,
        behind the thick clear glass of the mason jar. We watched

how they crawled, stingers readied, on top of one another, circling.
        Our discovery felt awful, like unearthing mortality.

We were two girls then, and despite our restless fear
        we could not bring ourselves to kill them, we grew almost

fond of the way they scurried against the glass, the way they became
        almost ours—minuscule marauders, all things of the night captured

in the light's unforgiving reveal. We do not know what happened to them.
We left the scorplings in the middle of the floor in the glass with a sign

that said, simply, *Jar of Scorpions*. This is where it ends. Or begins.
What do you want for them? From here, we can make it up.

THE FIRST FISH

When I pulled that great fish up out of Lake Skinner's
      mirrored-double surface, I wanted to release
the tugging beast immediately. Disaster on the rod,
      it seemed he might yank the whole aluminum skiff
down toward the bottom of his breathless world.
      The old tree of a man yelled to hang on and would
not help me as I reeled and reeled, finally seeing
      the black carp come up to meet me, black eye
to black eye. In the white cooler it looked so impossible.
      Is this where I am supposed to apologize? Not
only to the fish, but to the whole lake, land, not only for me
      but for the generations of plunder and vanish.
I remember his terrible mouth opening as if to swallow
      the barbarous girl he'd lose his life to. That gold-ringed
eye did not pardon me, no absolution, no reprieve.
      I wanted to catch something; it wanted to live.
We never ate the bottom-feeder, buried by the rosebush
      where my ancestors swore the roses bloomed
twice as big that year, the year I killed a thing because
      I was told to, the year I met my twin and buried
him without weeping so I could be called brave.

JOINT CUSTODY

Why did I never see it for what it was:
abundance? Two families, two different
kitchen tables, two sets of rules, two
creeks, two highways, two stepparents
with their fish tanks or eight-tracks or
cigarette smoke or expertise in recipes or
reading skills. I cannot reverse it, the record
scratched and stopping to that original
chaotic track. But let me say, I was taken
back and forth on Sundays and it was not easy
but I was loved each place. And so I have
two brains now. Two entirely different brains.
The one that always misses where I'm not,
and the one that is so relieved to finally be home.

ON SKYLINE AND TAR

At eleven on the rooftop
of our downtown apartment
building, I'd sit cross-legged
in the civil twilight's crawl

and wait for the pallid bats
to come out from their
pink roosts in the Sebastiani
Theatre into the pale sky.

We were taught to stay
small and watch how they
swerved and flickered free
in a secret dark spectacle.

How unexpectedly they
plummeted and rose and rose
and plummeted. Trouble came
and trouble left and the sky—

CYRUS & THE SNAKES

My brother holds a snake by its head. The whole
      length of the snake is the length

of my brother's body. The snake's head
      is held safely, securely, as if my brother

is showing it something in the distant high grass.
      I don't know why he wants to hold them,

their strong bodies wrapping themselves around
      the warmth of his arm. Constricting and made

of circles and momentum; slippery coolness smooth
      against the ground. Still, this image of him,

holding a snake as it snakes as snakes
      do, both a noun and a verb and a story

that doesn't end well. Once, we stole an egg
      from the backyard chicken coop

and cracked it just to see what was inside: a whole
      unhatched chick. Where we

expected yolk and mucus was an unfeathered
      and unfurled sweetness. We stared at the thing,

dead now and unshelled by curiosity and terrible youth.
      My brother pretended not to care so much,

while I cried, though only a little. Still, we buried it
        in the brush, by the creeping thistle that tore up

our arms with their speared leaves, barbed
        at the ends like weapons stuck in the rattlesnake grass.

But I knew, I knew that he'd cry if he was alone,
        if he wasn't a boy in the summer heat being a boy

in the summer heat. Years later, back from Mexico
        or South America, he'd admit he was tired

of history, of always discovering the ruin by ruining
        it, wrecking a forest for a temple, a temple

that should be simply left a temple. He wanted it
        all to stay as it was, even if it went undiscovered.

I want to honor a man who wants to hold a wild thing,
        only for a second, long enough to admire it fully,

and then wants to watch it safely return to its life,
        bends to be sure the grass closes up behind it.

ONLY THE FAINTEST BLUE

Somewhere in the haunted desert
I hitched my callow life to a man

who thought I hadn't suffered enough.
He might have said that very thing,

You haven't suffered enough. Young
whiptail lizards lined the cottonwood

path to the river where I walked each
day to remember who I was: *She*

who had not suffered. My hands tanned
in the sage-green air, I walked until

I was softer, until clouds, until I could
tame my colors and go back and cook

a lazy dinner. Once, he insisted I ride
home with a friend who was clearly drunk

so he could make a call he didn't
want me to hear—an ex, a lawyer, a dealer,

I don't know. I knew I didn't like his friend,
who drove too fast after shots of tequila

at the roadside Mexican dive with fake
spiky cacti in the foyer like stage props.

Maybe this is suffering? I thought.
Am I suffering now? Or now?

I felt most myself by the river. Vast
sorrel river ready to flood or tear down

everything in its way, hard to cross,
rapid and legendary. The color of the earth.

I did not want to throw myself in. Instead
I'd watch the whiptails skitter in dust.

Sisters of the small quiet pleasure of edges
and disappearing to safety. I can still hear

that river in my mind, my teacher, can still
remember the day I left him, the arguing,

the fight where I kept my head down
and packed like fury was a new smart skill.

But mostly I remember the flitting of lizards,
how they had felt like kinship,

how later, I read that the New Mexico whiptail
is an all-female species, reproducing by

parthenogenesis, asexual and yet genetically diverse.
Yellow lines run the length of their gray bodies

with vibrant blue-green tails when they're young.
And as they age, their scales, their whole body changes,

until only the faintest blue remains, and safer now,
they become the earthen color of the river.

CALLING THINGS WHAT THEY ARE

I pass the feeder and yell, *Grackle party!* And then an hour later I yell, *Mourning dove afterparty!* (I call the feeder the party and the seed on the ground the afterparty.) I am getting so good at watching that I've even dug out the binoculars an old poet gave me back when I was young and heading to the Cape with so much future ahead of me it was like my own ocean. *Tufted titmouse!* I yell, and Lucas laughs and says, *Thought so.* But he is humoring me; he didn't think so at all. My father does this same thing. Shouts out at the feeder announcing the party attendees. He throws out a whole peanut or two to the Steller's jay who visits on a low oak branch in the morning. To think there was a time I thought birds were kind of boring. Brown bird. Gray bird. Black bird. Blah blah blah bird. Then, I started to learn their names by the ocean, and the person I was dating said, *That's the problem with you, Limón, you're all fauna and no flora.* And I began to learn the names of trees. I like to call things as they are. Before, the only thing I was interested in was love, how it grips you, how it terrifies you, how it annihilates and resuscitates you. I didn't know then that it wasn't even love that I was interested in but my own suffering. I thought suffering kept things interesting. How funny that I called it love and the whole time it was pain.

"I HAVE WANTED CLARITY IN LIGHT OF MY LACK OF LIGHT"

After Alejandra Pizarnik

Fireworks in the background like an incongruous soundtrack,
    either celebratory or ominous, a veil of smoke behind

a neighbor's house, the air askew with booms.

The silver suitcase is dragged down the stairs, a clunk, another clunk,
    awkward wheels where wheels aren't any use. Uselessness of invention.

There is a knocking in the blood that is used to absence but hates this part
    the most. The sudden buried hope of illusion.

Lose my number, sadness. Lose my address, my storm door, my skull.

Am I stronger or weaker than when the year began, a lie
    that joins two selves like a hinge. Sawdust in the neighbor's garage

that smells of the men who raised me. What is the other world
    that others live in? Unknown to me. The ease of grin and good times.

Once, I loved fireworks so much they made me weep without warning.
    I smoked too much pot one young summer and almost missed them

until I simply remembered to look up. Gold valley crackling in chaos.

Now, it is a sound that undoes me, too much violence to the sky.
    In this way, I have become more dog. More senses, shake, and nerve.

Better now when the etches in the night's edges are just bats,
       erratic and avoiding the fireflies. How much more drama

can one body take? I wake up in the morning and relinquish my dreams.
       I go to bed with my beloved. I am delirious with my tenderness.

Once, I was brave, but I have grown so weary of danger.
       I am soundlessness amid the constant sounds of war.

OPEN WATER

It does no good to trick and weave and lose
the other ghosts, to shove the buried deeper
into the sandy loam, the riverine silt; still you come,
my faithful one, the sound of a body so persistent
in water I cannot tell if it is a wave or you
moving through. A month before you died
you wrote a letter to old friends saying you swam
with a pod of dolphins in open water, saying goodbye,
but what you told me most about was the eye.
That enormous reckoning eye of an unknown fish
that passed you during that last-ditch defiant swim.
On the shore, you described the fish as nothing
you'd seen before, a blue-gray behemoth moving slowly
and enduringly through its deep fathomless
North Pacific waters. That night, I heard more
about that fish and that eye than anything else.
I don't know why it has come to me this morning.
Warm rain and landlocked, I don't deserve the image.
But I keep thinking how something saw you, something
was bearing witness to you out there in the ocean
where you were no one's mother, and no one's wife,
but you in your original skin; right before you died,
you were beheld, and today in my kitchen with you
now ten years gone, I am so happy for you.

THORNS

Armed with our white plastic buckets
we set off in the safety of the noonday
heat to snag the full rubus blackberries
at the bend of her family's gravel road.
But before we even reached the end
of the driveway, a goose hung strangled
in the fence wire, bloodless and limp. Her
long neck twisted, her hard beak open.
She was dead. Though we had been loosed
like loyal ranch dogs, we knew we should
go back, tell someone, offer help. Still,
sunburned and stubborn in the way only
long free days can make a body, we walked
to the thicket and picked. When we returned,
bloodied by prickles and spattered with stains,
we were scolded, not for secreting
the news of the dead goose, but for picking
too many berries. For picking all day
in the sun without worry for our own scratched
skin. I can still remember how satisfying
it was. How we picked in near silence, two
girls who were never silent. How we knew
to plunder so well, to take and take
with this new muscle, this new gristle
that grew over us for good.

THE MOUNTAIN LION

I watched the video clip over and over,
night vision cameras flickering her eyes
an unholy green, the way she looked
the six-foot fence up and down
like it was nothing but a speed bump,
then cleared the man-made border
in one impressive leap. A glance
over the shoulder, an annoyance,
an *As if you could keep me out, or*
keep me in. I don't know what it
was that made me press replay and
replay. Not fear, though I'd be
terrified if I was face to face with
her, or heard her prowling in the night.
It was just that I don't think I've
ever made anything look so easy. Never
looked behind me and grinned or
grimaced because nothing could stop
me. I like the idea of it though, felt
like a dream you could will into being:
See a fence? Jump it.

3.
FALL

PRIVACY

On the black wet branches of the linden,
still clinging to the umber leaves of late fall,
two crows land. They say, *Stop*, and still I want
to make them into something they are not.
Odin's ravens, the bruja's eyes. What news
are they bringing of our world to the world
of the gods? It can't be good. More suffering
all around, more stinging nettles and toxic
blades shoved into the scarred parts of us,
the minor ones underneath the trees. Rain
comes while I'm still standing, a trickle of water
from whatever we believe is beyond the sky.
The crows seem enormous but only because
I am watching them too closely. They do not
care to be seen as symbols. A shake of a wing,
and both of them are gone. There was no message
given, no message I was asked to give, only
their great absence and my sad privacy
returning like the bracing, empty wind
on the black wet branches of the linden.

IT'S THE SEASON I OFTEN MISTAKE

Birds for leaves, and leaves for birds.
The tawny yellow mulberry leaves
are always goldfinches tumbling
across the lawn like extreme elation.
The last of the maroon crabapple
ovates are song sparrows that tremble
all at once. And today, just when I
could not stand myself any longer,
a group of field sparrows, which were
actually field sparrows, flew up into
the bare branches of the hackberry
and I almost collapsed: leaves
reattaching themselves to the tree
like a strong spell for reversal. What
else did I expect? What good
is accuracy amidst the perpetual
scattering that unspools the world.

HOW WE SEE EACH OTHER

I forget I am a woman walking alone and wave
      at a maroon car, assuming it's a neighbor or a friend.

The car then circles the block and goes past me five times.
      One wave and five times the car circles. Strangers.

It is the early evening, the fireflies not yet out,
      I trick the hunting car by pretending to walk into

a different house. I am upset by this, but it is life, so I make
      dinner and listen to a terrible audiobook on Latin American

literature that's so dull it's Dove soap. Violence is done and history
      records it. Gold ruins us. Men ruin us.

That's how the world
was made, don't you know?

A group of us, to tune out grief every week, are watching
      dance movies. Five women watching people leap and grind.

Every time I watch the films, I cry. Each week, even though
      we are hidden from each other by distance, I know

I am the first to break into tears. Something about the body
      moving freely, someone lifting it, or just the body

alone in movement, safe in the black expanse of stage. The body
      as rebellion, as defiance, as immune.

Aracelis writes to tell me she's had a dream where
        I am in Oaxaca wearing a black dress covered with animals.

In her dream I am brushing and brushing my hair with a brush
        made out of animal hair. There is a large mirror and a room

        full of books.
History comes at us through the sheen of time.

I write back, *Was it ominous or was it hopeful?*
She says, *The word I am thinking of is "strong."*

I kindle the image in my body all day, the mirror, the brush,
        the animals, the vast space of the imagination,

the solid gaze of a woman who has witnessed me as unassailable,
        the clarity of her vision so clean I feel almost free.

SPORTS

I've seen my fair share of baseball games,
eaten smothered hot dogs in Kansas City
and carne asada burritos in San Francisco
in the sunny stands on a day free of fog.
I've sat in a bar for hours watching
basketball and baseball and the Super Bowl,
and I've even high-fived and clinked
my almost-empty drink with a stranger
because it felt good to go through something
together even though we hadn't been through
anything but the drama of a game, its players.
If I am honest, what I love, why I love
the sounds of the games even when I'm not
interested, half-listening, is one thing:
When my father and my stepfather had to be
in the same room, or had to drop my brother
and me off during our weekly move from one
house to another, they, for a brief moment,
would stand together in the doorway or
on the gravel driveway and it felt like what true
terror should feel like, two men who were so
different you could barely see their shadows
attached in the same way, and just when
I thought I couldn't watch the pause
lengthen between them, they'd talk about
the playoffs or the finals or whatever team
was doing whatever thing required that season
and sometimes they'd even shrug or make
a motion that felt like two people who weren't
opposites after all. Once, I sat in the car

and waited for one of them to take me away
and from the back seat I swear they looked
like they were on the same team, united
against a common enemy, had been fighting,
all this time, on the same side.

PROOF

A kestrel eyes us from a high thin branch
and my husband is surprised it can hold the hunter's
weight. *He's small*, I say. My husband says he's large.
Obviously, it depends on what you compare him to—
a hawk, a white-crowned sparrow, a ghost,
an abstraction. He looms not large to me, but significant.
A standout. Something cool about him that says today
is the day to test his mettle in the mid-morning air,
flush with dead leaves and the ongoingness of rusted
mums. A surge of relief comes like a check in the mail.
Look, I have already witnessed something other than my
slipping face in the fogged mirror, the dog's sweet
seriousness at being worshipped from nose to paw.
I have proof a nearly twiglike branch can still hold
a too-heavy falcon. It is not much to go on, I know.

HEART ON FIRE

As a foster child, my grandfather learned not
to get in trouble. Mexican and motherless—dead
as she was from tuberculosis—he practiced words
in a new language and kept his slender head down.
When the other boys begged him to slip into
the music shop's upper window to steal harmonicas
for each of them, music being important, thievery
being secondary, he refused. When the cops came
to spot the boys who robbed the music store, they
could easily find the ones spitting broken
notes into the air, joyously mouthing the stainless
steel, mimicking men on street corners busking
for coins. But not my grandfather, he knew not
to risk it all for a stolen moment of exultation.
It's easy to imagine this is who I come from, a line
of serious men who follow the rules, but might I add
that later he was a dancer, a singer, an actor whose best roles
ended up on the cutting room floor. A cutup, a ham
who liked a good story. Who would have told you
life was a series of warnings, but also magic. Once,
he was sent for a box of matches and he put that box
of strike-anywheres in the pocket of his madras shirt
and ran home, he ran so fast to be on time, to be good,
and when he did so, the whole box ignited, so he was
a boy running down the canyon road with what
looked like a heart on fire. He'd laugh when he told
you this, *a heart on fire*, he'd say, so you'd remember.

POWER LINES

Three guys in fluorescent vests are taking down
a tree along my neighbor's fence line, which is, of course,

my fence line, with my two round-eyed snakes and my wandering

raccoon. That is, if you go in for ownership. *My, my, my.*
For weeks the tree they're cutting grew tight with a neon-pink band

around its trunk. A marking, so you knew it was going to die.

Must have been at least fifty years old, a nonfruiting
mulberry with loads of wintercreeper crawling up the bark.

Still it hung low by the power lines. Its fruitless limbs

leaning over the wire like it didn't care one bit about power.
Just inching up toward the sun under the hackberry.

The men are laughing between chain saw growls,

the metal jaws of machinery. It is a sound that sounds like killing.
I can barely listen, but then they are conversing in Spanish

and it brings me a mercy to hear them make a joke

about the heat, the lineup of jobs that day. Once,
my friend Mundo wanted palm fronds for his patio

so he put on an orange shirt and climbed a towering palm

right in the center of town. *No one ever questions a Mexican
in an orange shirt*, he said, and we clinked glasses around

his new tiki bar. My grandfather worked for Con Edison for years.

I thought power was something you could control. Something one
could do at a desk or on a job site, to work in the field of power.

Now the tree is gone. The men are gone, just a ground-down stump
where what felt like wisdom once was.

HOOKY

We skipped that last class, rolled
joints in my clean apartment close to a bar
called Flowers, which we loved and went
to so often that once, Joel's dad found
his maxed-out credit card statement and said,
*Who are you buying all these flowers
for?* That day we weren't bound
for the bar, where Fadi kept a back table
for friends and on busy nights let us hover.
It was a rare Brigadoon day when the sun
bared herself in Seattle's U District and the trees
were in heat and everything felt wild and illicit
and we decided to get as high as we could
and lie down under the cherry trees. I was
straight As and dean's list, but could roll
three perfect joints and even add a filter
thanks to three guys I met in a Spanish hostel.
And when we made it to that kaleidoscopic
row of ancient cherry trees we started laughing
hard and scary like, contagious, and the breeze
was blowing pink cherry blossoms through the air
and everyone we saw was stoned and making
out with someone and it seemed so absurd
that we would ever learn anything from inside
the darkness and soon it wasn't so much funny
anymore but serious. The true and serious beauty
of trees, how it seemed insane that they should
offer this to us, how unworthy we were, bewildered,

how soon we were nearly weeping at their trunks
as they tossed down petal after petal, and we tried
to remember how it felt to receive and notice
the receiving, pink, pink, pink, pink, pink.

MY FATHER'S MUSTACHE

Let us pause to applaud the white bell-bottom suit,
the wide flared collar, the black thick-coiffed hair
in this photo my father has sent of himself
at a gathering off Sonoma Highway in the early '70s.
I can't stop looking at the photo. There is a swagger
that feels almost otherworldly, epic, like Lorca
expounding in Buenos Aires, *Not the form*
but the marrow of form. He is perfect there, my father
in the photo. I feel somehow as if I'm perched on a bay laurel
branch nearby though not born yet. It's in black and white, the photo.
You can see his grin behind his lush mustache. Is it time
that moves in me now? A sense of ache and unraveling,
my father in his pristine white suit, the eye of the world barely able
to handle his smooth unbroken stride. It's been a year
since I've seen him in person, I miss how he points
to his apple trees and I miss his smooth face
that no longer has the mustache I always adored.
As a child I once cried when he shaved it. Even then,
I was too attached to this life.

RUNAWAY CHILD

The ocean was two things once,
         in two places, north it was the high

icy waves of Bodega Bay, Dillon, and Limantour,
         and south it was the blue ease

of Oceanside and Encinitas, umbrellas
         in a sleepy breeze.

It took me years to realize those two blues
         were the same ocean.

I thought they must be separate. Must
         be cleaved in the center by a fault line.

On a call just now with my grandmother
         she mentions how all the flowers

I've sent are from my garden, so I let her
         believe it. Sweet lies of the mind.

She says she's surprised
         I like to grow things, didn't think

I was that kind of girl, she always thought I was
         a runaway child.

She flicks her hand away, to show me
         her hand becoming a bird, swerving

until it is a white gull in the wind. She repeats:
     a runaway child.

Mercy is not frozen in time, but flits
     about frantically, unsure where to land.

As children, they'd bring us to the ocean,
     divorce distraction and summer,

we'd drift with the tide southward until
     we'd almost lose sight of them,

waving dramatically for our return,
     shouting until we came back to shore.

Once, when she was watching us,
     I tried to run away, four or five years old,

and when I got to the end of the driveway,
     she didn't try to stop me. Even shut the door.

And so I came back. She knew what it was
     to be unloved, abandoned by her mother,

riding her bike by her father's house
     with his other children, late afternoons,

before her grandmother would call
     her home for supper. Some days, I think

she would have let me leave, some days
     I think of her shaking on the shore.

Now, she thinks all the flowers I've sent
    are from my garden. Grown

from seeds and tended. She gets a kick
    out of it, this runaway child

so overly loved, she could dare to drift
    away from it all.

INSTRUMENTATION

If I could ever play an instrument for real I like the idea of playing the jawbone, that rattle of something dead in your hands, that thing that beats back at the sky and says, *I'm still here,* even though clearly the donkey isn't here or the horse isn't here, just the teeth and the jaw making music like resurrection or haunting or just plain need. What I like most is that the jawbone is an idiophone, which I misread once as *ideaphone.* But an *idiophone* is just that it makes music by the whole thing vibrating without strings. I want that. That kind of reeling in the wind. All the loose dry teeth, all the old bones of the skull, all the world, and the figure swaying with its stick to make untuned music even death cannot deny.

IF I SHOULD FAIL

The ivy eating the fence line,
each tendril multiplying
by green tendril, if I should
fail the seeds lifted out
and devoured by bristled
marauders, blame only
me and the strip of sun
which bade me come
to lie down snakelike
on my belly, low snake
energy, and be tempted
by the crevices between
the world and not world,
if I should fail know I
stared long into fractures
and it seemed to me
a mighty system of gaps
one could slither into
and I was made whole
in that knowledge of
a sleek nothingness.

INTIMACY

I remember watching my mother
with the horses, the cool, fluid
way she'd guide those enormous
bodies around the long field,
the way she'd shoulder one aside
if it got too close, if it got greedy
with the alfalfa or apple.
I was never like that. Never
so confident around those
four-legged giants who could
kill with one kick or harm
with one toss of their strong heads.
To me, it didn't make sense
to trust a thing that could
destroy you so quickly, to reach
out your hand and stroke
the deep separateness
of a beast, that long gap
of silence between you,
knowing it would eat the apples
with as much pleasure from
any flattened palm. Is that why
she moved with them so easily?
There is a truth in that smooth
indifference, a clean honesty
about our otherness that feels
not like the moral but the story.

4.
WINTER

LOVER

Easy light storms in through the window, soft
      edges of the world, smudged by mist, a squirrel's

      nest rigged high in the maple. I've got a bone
to pick with whoever is in charge. All year,

I've said, *You know what's funny?* and then,
      Nothing, nothing is funny. Which makes me laugh

      in an oblivion-is-coming sort of way. A friend
writes the word *lover* in a note and I am strangely

excited for the word *lover* to come back. Come back,
      lover, come back to the five-and-dime. I could

      squeal with the idea of blissful release, oh lover,
what a word, what a world, this gray waiting. In me,

a need to nestle deep into the safekeeping of sky.
      I am too used to nostalgia now, a sweet escape

      of age. Centuries of pleasure before us and after
us, still right now, a softness like the worn fabric of a nightshirt,

and what I do not say is: I trust the world to come back.
      Return like a word, long forgotten and maligned

      for all its gross tenderness, a joke told in a sunbeam,
the world walking in, ready to be ravaged, open for business.

THE HURTING KIND

I.

On the plane I have a dream I've left half my
        torso on the back porch with my beloved. I have to go

back for it, but it's too late, I'm flying
        and there's only half of me.

Back in Texas, the flowers I've left on
        the counter (I stay alone there so the flowers
are more than flowers) have wilted and knocked over the glass.

At the funeral parlor with my mother, we are holding her father's suit,
        and she says, *He'll swim in these.*

For a moment, I'm not sure what she means,

until I realize she means the clothes are too big.

I go with her like a shield in case they try to upsell her
        the ridiculously ornate urn, the elaborate body box.

It is a nice bathroom in the funeral parlor,
        so I take the opportunity to change my tampon.

When I come out my mother says,
Did you have to change your tampon?

And it seems, all at once, a vulgar life. Or not
        vulgar, but not simple, either.

I'm driving her now to Hillside Cemetery where we meet
        with Rosie, who is so nice we want her to work
everywhere. Rosie as my dentist. Rosie as my president.

My shards are showing, I think. But I do not know what I mean
so I fix my face in the rearview, a face with thousands
        of headstones behind it. Minuscule flags, plastic flowers.

        You can't sum it up, my mother says as we are driving,
and the electronic voice says, *Turn left onto Wildwood Canyon Road,*

so I turn left, happy for the instructions.

Tell me where to go. Tell me how to get there.

She means a life, of course. You cannot sum it up.

2.

A famous poet said he never wanted to hear
another poem about a grandmother or a grandfather.

I imagine him with piles of faded yolk-colored paper,
overloaded with loops of swooping cursive, anemic lyrics

misspelling *mourning* and *morning*. But also, before they arrive,
there's a desperate hand scribbling a memory, following

the cat of imagination into each room. What is lineage,
if not a gold thread of pride and guilt? *She did what?*

Once, when I thought I had decided not to have children,
a woman said, *But who are you to kill your own bloodline?*

I told my friend D that, and she said, *What if you want to kill
your own bloodline, like it's your job?*

In the myth of La Llorona, she drowns her children
to destroy her cheating husband. But maybe she was just tired.

After her husband of seventy-six years has died, my grandmother
(yes, I said it, *grandmother, grandmother*) leans to me and says,

Now teach me poetry.

3.

Sticky packs of photographs,
heteromaniacal postcards.

The war.   The war.   The war.
Bikini girls, tight curls, the word *gams*.

Land boom. Atchison, Topeka,
and the Santa Fe. Southern Pacific.

We ask my grandma Allamay
about her mother, for a form.

Records and wills. Evidence of life.
For a moment she can't remember
her mother's maiden name.

She says, *Just tell them she never*
wanted me. That should be enough.

Red sadness is the secret
one, writes Ruefle. Redlands

was named after the soil.
Allamay can still
hold a peach in her hand

and judge its number by
its size. Tell you where it
would go in the box

if you're packing peaches
for a living. Which she did,

though she hated the way
the hairs hurt her hands.

4.

Why do we quickly dismiss our ancient ones? Before our phones
         stole the light of our faces, shiny and blue in the televised night,

they worked farms and butchered and trapped animals and swept houses
         and returned to each other after long hours and told stories.

In order for someone to be "good" do they have to have
         seen the full-tilt world? Must they believe what we believe?

My grandmother keeps a picture of her president in the top drawer
       of her dresser, and once, when she was delusional, she dreamt

he had sent my grandfather and her on a trip to Italy. *He paid for it all,*
       she kept repeating.

That same night, on her ride to the hospital, she talks to the medical
       technician and says,

All my grandchildren are Mexican.

She says so proudly; she repeats it to me on the phone.

5.

Once, a long time ago, we sat in the carport of my grandparents'
       house in Redlands, now stolen by eminent domain,

now the hospital parking lot, no more coyotes or caves
       where the coyotes would live, or the grandfather clock

in the house my grandfather built, the porch above the orchard,
       all gone.

We sat in the carport and watched the longest snake
       I'd ever seen undulate between the hanging succulents.

They told me not to worry, that the snake had a name,

       the snake was called a California king,

all slick black with yellow
       stripes like wonders wrapping around him.

My grandparents, my ancestors, told me never
       to kill a California king, benevolent

as they were, equanimous like earth or sky, not

       toothy like the dog Chacho who barked
at nearly every train whistle or roadrunner.

Before my grandfather died, I asked him what sort
       of horse he had growing up. He said,

Just a horse. My horse, with such a tenderness it
       rubbed the bones in my ribs all wrong.

I have always been too sensitive, a weeper
       from a long line of weepers.

I am the hurting kind. I keep searching for proof.

My grandfather carried that snake to the cactus,
       where all sharp things could stay safe.

6.

You can't sum it up. A life.

I feel it moving through me, that snake,
       his horse Midge sturdy and nothing special,

traveling the canyons and the tumbleweeds
        hunting for rabbits before the war.

My grandmother picking peaches. Stealing
        the fruit from the orchards as she walked

home. No one said it was my job to remember.

        I took no notes, though I've stared too long.
My grandfather, before he died, would have told

        anyone that could listen that he was ordinary,

that his life was a good one, simple, he could never
        understand why anyone would want to write

it down. He would tell you straight up he wasn't
        brave. And my grandmother would tell you right now

that he is busy getting the house ready for her. Visiting now
each night and even doing the vacuuming.

I imagine she's right. It goes on and on, their story.
        They met in first grade in a one-room schoolhouse,

I could have started their story there, but it
        is endless and ongoing. All of this

is a conjuring. I will not stop this reporting of attachments.
        There is evidence everywhere.

There's a tree over his grave now, and soon her grave too

though she is tough and says, *If I ever die,*

which is marvelous and maybe why she's still alive.

I see the tree above the grave and think, *I'm wearing*

my heart on my leaves. My heart on my leaves.

Love ends. But what if it doesn't?

AGAINST NOSTALGIA

If I had known, back then, you were coming,
when I first thought love could be the thing
to save me after all—if I had known, would I
have still glued myself to the back of his
motorcycle while we flew across the starless
bridge over the East River to where I grew
my first garden behind the wire fencing,
in the concrete raised beds lined by ruby
twilight roses? If I had known it would be you,
who even then I liked to look at, across a room,
always listening rigorously, a self-questioning look,
the way your mouth was always your mouth,
would I have climbed back on that bike again
and again until even I was sick with fumes
and the sticky seat too hot in the early fall?
If I had known, would I have still made mistake
after mistake until I had only the trunk of me
left, stripped and nearly bare of leaves?
If I had known, the truth is, I would have kneeled
and said, *Sooner, come to me sooner.*

FORGIVENESS

It was the winter of manatees, Captain
      Rhonda and her chartered pontoon boat
floating down the Crystal River. It was the winter

you hurt me and that day of dumb hearts
      when you brought me truffles and perfume
like a performance. At the tiki bar in the cold

February Florida wind, Rihanna played over
      the staticky speakers hidden
behind a fake coconut, something about giving up

or saying something. At the restaurant later, the couple
      we laughed at, in their late fifties, for maybe being
swingers, all the uniform tables, identical roses

in cheap plastic vases. Even my deep cleavage
      and the layer cake were trying too hard. Still, we
committed to the event of us and made a joke

about not hurting each other again. We weren't
      married yet, everyone was free to leave, and the next
afternoon you went to work and I took a boat

down the river to see the manatees. It was back
      when I got lonely often, I called and asked
if I could bring my dog on the boat. I couldn't.

So tranquil and patient, the manatees moving, so many
        mysteries even in the shallow water. Captain
Rhonda showed us their hideouts, their shadowy places.

People took pictures and pointed and you could see
        the scars on the older animals from propeller blades
and still they rolled on together in the silent water.

Back on shore, you found me by the too-cold pool
        watching a group of loud teenagers drink
in the hot tub. One shirtless boy kept flexing and flexing

while the girls, engrossed in conversation, never noticed.
        And aren't we all alone in the end?
You put your head for a moment against my chest.

Then, all I could hear was our breathing. We were
        both human and animal-hearted,
bound to the blades, bound to outrun them.

HEAT

The icicles dripped and sharpened
in my bones. Even my sick dark
mood was shiny like glass,
breakable and almost decorative.
In my world of brittle needles,
I was building my house of ice,
brick by brick and fastened by
sullenness. Then, like a huge feral
animal, you stomped down
the stairs to the ground floor where
I sulked. I did not look up
to see you, talking as you
were on the phone with a comrade
about a horse, or the snow,
or the snow light and how
it reflected on the horse,
and you were all business and I
was all business until I looked
toward you and you, like
some freshly baptized sinner,
were naked, still wet from the shower,
barefoot, bare, and dripping,
and from where I was kneeling
I was made aware of your fineness.
Your body I thought belonged to me,
until I learned about belonging,
was sublime, looming over me
like a gauntlet, and because
you were a challenge, I rose
from the cold to meet you.

OBEDIENCE

The dog lifts her head
from the piles of dead
leaves, and at first she
is calm, until she is not.
She can't find me. Not
behind the cypress or
the still-bare viburnum.
Betrayer, I am watching
from the window. Warm
behind the doorframe.
What is it to be wholly
loved like this? God,
how desperate she is
to find me. Walking
toward her, I watch her
whole body vibrate
when I come into focus.
I lift her into my arms
because it is what
I want. Who doesn't want
to hold their individual
god, to be redeemed by
pleasing the only
one you serve?

THE UNSPOKEN

If I'm honest, a foal pulled chest-level
close in the spring heat, his every-which-way
coat reverberating in the wind, feels
akin to what I imagine atonement might
feel like, or total absolution. But what
if, by some fluke in the heart, an inevitable
wreckage, congenital and unanswerable,
still comes, no matter how attached
or how gentle every hand that reached
out for him in that vibrant green field
where they found him looking like he
was sleeping, the mare nudging him
until she no longer nudged him? Am I
wrong to say I did not want to love
horses after that? I even said as much driving
back from the farm. Even now, when
invited to visit a new foal, or rub the long
neck of a mare who wants only peppermints
or to be left alone, I feel myself resisting.
At any moment, something terrible could
happen. It's not gone, that coldness in me.
Our mare is pregnant right now,
and you didn't even tell me until someone
mentioned it offhandedly. One day, I will
be stronger. I feel it coming. I'll step into
that green field stoic, hardened, hoof first.

SALVAGE

On the top of Mount Pisgah, on the western
slope of the Mayacamas, there's a madrone
tree that's half-burned from the fires, half-alive
from nature's need to propagate. One side
of her is black ash, and at her root is what
looks like a cavity hollowed out by flame.
On the other side, silvery-green broadleaf
shoots ascend toward the winter light
and her bark is a cross between a bay
horse and a chestnut horse, red and velvety
like the animal's neck she resembles. Staring
at the tree for a long time now, I am reminded
of the righteousness I had before the scorch
of time. I miss who I was. I miss who we all were,
before we were this: half-alive to the brightening sky,
half-dead already. I place my hand on the unscarred
bark that is cool and unsullied, and because I cannot
apologize to the tree, to my own self I say, *I am sorry.*
I am sorry I have been so reckless with your life.

WHAT IS HANDED DOWN

Smoke and sweat seeped through
your waiter's vest, and nights off you'd play
the harmonica on the rooftop, a man made
out of netting and wire with an unexpected
tenor, made of push-ups and the sound
of typewriter keys, eight-tracks and knowing
all the lyrics to all the songs. I thought you were
a celebrity, the way people shouted your name
when we walked though the plaza. Even as a child,
I noticed your gentle way of fixing. The first time
I saw it, it felt like a trick. The spider plant I killed
because I didn't care enough about lives other than
my own was soaked in the apartment sink until
it came back to life. My mother's clock radio you took
apart and put back together good as new, though
the war had made it so you couldn't hear
the high notes. It's selfish, I know, but I want to be
the fixer now. Show me how you did it, all those years,
took something that needed repair and repaired it.

TOO CLOSE

Shiny little knives of ice
        have replaced the grass
and yes they seem like
        blades now more than
any other time before,
        they are sharp needles
erupting from the ground
        and poor grass, covered
as it is and so cold. In
        the near distance, a tree
falls, or large branches,
        a roar that sounds as
violent as it is when later
        the poor downed Callery pear
divided almost in two,
        one part of the trunk
on the ground and another
        somehow continuing on.
I could not do any of these
        things. In winter, a distance
grows, the world was
        breathing, and then suddenly
it was not. *Pyrus calleryana* breaks
        easily because it keeps
its leaves and is known
        to split apart in storms.
But haven't we learned by now
        that just because something
is bound to break
        doesn't mean we shouldn't
shiver when it breaks?

THE END OF POETRY

Enough of osseous and chickadee and sunflower
and snowshoes, maple and seeds, samara and shoot,
enough chiaroscuro, enough of thus and prophecy
and the stoic farmer and faith and our father and 'tis
of thee, enough of bosom and bud, skin and god
not forgetting and star bodies and frozen birds,
enough of the will to go on and not go on or how
a certain light does a certain thing, enough
of the kneeling and the rising and the looking
inward and the looking up, enough of the gun,
the drama, and the acquaintance's suicide, the long-lost
letter on the dresser, enough of the longing and
the ego and the obliteration of ego, enough
of the mother and the child and the father and the child
and enough of the pointing to the world, weary
and desperate, enough of the brutal and the border,
enough of can you see me, can you hear me, enough
I am human, enough I am alone and I am desperate,
enough of the animal saving me, enough of the high
water, enough sorrow, enough of the air and its ease,
I am asking you to touch me.

NOTES & ACKNOWLEDGMENTS

My deepest appreciation goes to the friends, family, teachers, ghosts, ancestors, and mentors that these poems were written for, written with, written toward. I am made better for having listened to you, for your wisdom, for your kindness.

People who read these poems, sometimes daily and as soon as I sent them, deserve a medal for their generosity and patience. Thank you to Jennifer L. Knox, Jason Schneiderman, Matthew Zapruder, Rebecca Lindenberg, Adam Clay, Michael Robins, and my wonderful agent, Rob McQuilkin, who read and helped to edit the early versions of these poems.

These last years have been hard, grief-ridden, and isolated, and yet I've never been isolated because I've had these fine people in my corner. Thank you to Trish Harnetiaux and Heather Grossmann for always being there, for blowing on the wheel. Thank you to Vaughan Fielder for keeping me safe and keeping me going.

Thank you to Kristin Dombek, Dawn Lundy Martin, Stephanie Hopkins, and Nicole Callihan for your love and deadlines. Thank you to Camille Dungy, Major Jackson, Natalie Diaz, Dan Walinsky, Corey Stoll, Nadia Bowers, and Fred Leebron for your friendship and guidance. Thank you to Diana Lee Craig and Jeffrey Baker for your laughter and for my home on the mountain.

Thank you to Vanessa Holden, Mariama Lockington, Amanda Duckworth, and Hannah Pittard for keeping the light on during these dark times. Thank you to Cyrus, Emily, Bryce, and Dimitri Limón for keeping me grounded. Thank you to the poetry salon unicorns. Thank you to the Guggenheim Foundation for giving me support when I most needed it. Thank you to my students at various institutions for giving me hope. Thank you to the poets and poetry quoted here, including Alejandra Pizarnik, Federico García Lorca, Gabriela Mistral, Mary Ruefle, and Leonard Cohen. Thank you also, and always, to the trees and animals.

Thank you to Daniel Slager, Mary Austin Speaker, Joey McGarvey, Joanna Demkiewicz, Broc Rossell, and everyone at Milkweed Editions who makes and supports beautiful and necessary books. Thank you to Wayne Miller for your keen eye and big heart. Thank you to my publicist, Michael Taeckens, for your bright light.

Thank you to my father and Linda Limón for giving me the confidence and support to make poems. Thank you to my mother, Stacia Brady, for your incredible painting that graces the cover. Thank you to my stepfather, Brady T. Brady, who made this into the book it is and told me, very early on, never to give up on my poems. Finally, thank you to my love, Lucas Marquardt. I am so grateful to go through this life with you (and our animals, Lily Bean and Olive).

Thank you to the hardworking editors and fine publications where these poems, sometimes in earlier versions, first appeared:

Alone Together anthology: "Not the Saddest Thing in the World"

Alta: "Stillwater Cove," "Calling Things What They Are," "The First Lesson"

American Poetry Review: "It Begins with the Trees," "I Have Wanted Clarity in Light of My Lack of Light," "Banished Wonders," "In the Shadow, "The Magnificent Frigatebird"

Astra: "Blowing on the Wheel," "Against Nostalgia"

The Atlantic: "The Unspoken"

The Believer ("The Logger"): "Sports"

BOMB: "Hooky," "Proof"

Columbia Journal: "Stranger Things in the Thicket," "Swear on It," "On Skyline and Tar," "When It Comes Down to It"

Copper Nickel: "A Good Story"

Greenpeace: "Salvage"

Harvard Advocate: "The First Fish"

Jubilat: "Jar of Scorpions"

The Nation: "Drowning Creek"

New England Review: "Open Water"

New Republic: "My Father's Mustache"

New Yorker: "The End of Poetry," "Privacy"

Paris Review: "Power Lines"

Poem-a-Day: "Lover," "Give Me This"

Poetry Magazine: "Foaling Season"

Poetry Northwest: "Only the Faintest Blue," "Heart on Fire"

Pop-Up Magazine: "Thorns"

The Rumpus: "The Hurting Kind"

Sierra Club: "The Mountain Lion"

Thrush: "Cyrus & the Snakes"

Virginia Quarterly Review: "Intimacy," "Sanctuary," "Invasive," "Forsythia"

Washington Post: "It's the Season I Often Mistake"

Lucas Marquardt

ADA LIMÓN is the author of *The Hurting Kind*, as well as five other collections of poems. These include, most recently, *The Carrying*, which won the National Book Critics Circle Award and was named a finalist for the PEN/Jean Stein Book Award, and *Bright Dead Things*, which was named a finalist for the National Book Award, the National Book Critics Circle Award, and the Kingsley Tufts Award. Limón is a recipient of a Guggenheim Fellowship, and her work has appeared in the *New Yorker*, the *New York Times*, and *American Poetry Review*, among others. She is the host of American Public Media's week-day poetry podcast, *The Slowdown*. Born and raised in California, she now lives in Lexington, Kentucky.

milkweed
editions

Founded as a nonprofit organization in 1980, Milkweed Editions
is an independent publisher. Our mission is to identify, nurture
and publish transformative literature, and build
an engaged community around it.

Milkweed Editions is based in Bde Ota Othúŋwe (Minneapolis)
within Mni Sota Makočhe, the traditional homeland of the Dakota people.
Residing here since time immemorial, Dakota people still call Mni Sota
Makočhe home, with four federally recognized Dakota nations and many
more Dakota people residing in what is now the state of Minnesota.
Due to continued legacies of colonization, genocide, and forced removal,
generations of Dakota people remain disenfranchised from their traditional
homeland. Presently, Mni Sota Makočhe has become a refuge and home for
many Indigenous nations and peoples, including seven federally recognized
Ojibwe nations. We humbly encourage readers to reflect upon the historical
legacies held in the lands they occupy.

milkweed.org

Milkweed Editions also gratefully acknowledges sustaining support from our Board of Directors; the Alan B. Slifka Foundation and its president, Riva Ariella Ritvo-Slifka; the Amazon Literary Partnership; the Ballard Spahr Foundation; *Copper Nickel*; the McKnight Foundation; the National Endowment for the Arts; the National Poetry Series; the Target Foundation; and other generous contributions from foundations, corporations, and individuals. Also, this activity is made possible by the voters of Minnesota through a Minnesota State Arts Board Operating Support grant, thanks to a legislative appropriation from the arts and cultural heritage fund. For a full listing of Milkweed Editions supporters, please visit milkweed.org.

Typeset in Garamond
by Tijqua Daiker

Adobe Garamond is based upon the typefaces first created by Parisian printer Claude Garamond in the sixteenth century. Garamond based his typeface on the handwriting of Angelo Vergecio, librarian to King Francis I. The font's slenderness makes it not only highly readable but also one of the most eco-friendly typefaces available because it requires less ink than similar faces. Robert Slimbach created this digital version of Garamond for Adobe in 1989 and his font has become one of the most widely used typefaces in print.